Fuel Minds

Fuel Minds

Phase 7:
Daily Physical Fitness Routines

Wilbur N. Morris Jr

Fuel Minds LLC

TABLE OF CONTENTS

Welcome to "Fuel Minds: Phase 7 Daily Physical Fitness Routines", where we embark on a journey through the multifaceted world of daily physical fitness routines. This phase will explore various aspects of fitness and wellness, offering you a comprehensive guide to achieving a balanced and fulfilling fitness regimen. This phase provides the knowledge and tools to cultivate a healthy body and mind, from high-intensity functional training to mindfulness practices.

Exploring the Spectrum of Fitness

Physical fitness is not a one-size-fits-all concept. It encompasses various activities and practices catering to different preferences, goals, and lifestyles. This chapter will examine several popular and effective fitness methodologies, examining their unique benefits and potential risks. We aim to equip you with a well-rounded understanding of these practices, enabling you to make informed decisions about your fitness journey.

High-Intensity Functional Training

High-intensity functional training (HIFT) has gained immense popularity in recent years, and for good reason. This approach focuses on functional movements performed at high intensity, aiming to improve overall fitness and athletic performance. We will explore the principles of HIFT, including its benefits, such as enhanced cardiovascular health, increased strength, and improved metabolic function. Additionally, we will address the risks associated with high-intensity training and provide guidelines for safe and effective practice.

The World of CrossFit and Olympic Weightlifting

CrossFit and Olympic weightlifting are two prominent components of high-intensity functional training. This section will dive deeper into these disciplines, highlighting their core principles and techniques. CrossFit, known for its diverse and challenging workouts, combines cardio, weightlifting, and bodyweight exercises. We will discuss how CrossFit suits individuals of varying fitness levels and how to mitigate the risk of injury.

On the other hand, Olympic weightlifting emphasizes strength and power through two main lifts: the snatch and the clean and jerk. We will provide a detailed overview of these lifts, including proper form and technique, to help you safely incorporate Olympic weightlifting into your routine. Understanding the benefits of these lifts, such as increased muscle mass and improved coordination, will enable you to harness their full potential.

The Flexible World of Yoga

Yoga contrasts with high-intensity training, focusing on flexibility, balance, and mental well-being. In this section, we will explore the various styles of yoga, from the dynamic flows of Vinyasa to the meditative stillness of Yin yoga. Each style has its own set of benefits, and we will guide you in selecting the one that aligns best with your fitness goals and personal preferences.

In addition to physical benefits such as improved flexibility and reduced muscle tension, yoga promotes mental clarity and emotional stability. We will discuss how regular yoga can enhance mindfulness, reduce stress, and foster a deeper connection between mind and body.

Integrating Meditation and Breathing Exercises

Meditation and breathing exercises are powerful tools we will integrate into your daily fitness regimen. We will explore different meditation techniques, from mindfulness meditation to guided visualization, and explain how these practices can enhance your overall fitness experience.

Breathing exercises like diaphragmatic breathing and the 4-7-8 technique can improve respiratory function, reduce stress, and enhance focus. We will provide step-by-step instructions for incorporating these exercises into your daily routine, helping you achieve a state of calm and balance amidst the demands of modern life.

Conclusion

As we navigate through this phase, our goal is to present you with a holistic approach to fitness that encompasses both physical and mental well-being. Understanding the benefits and risks of various fitness practices and learning to integrate mindfulness techniques will empower you to create a daily routine that fuels your body, mind, and soul. Whether you are a seasoned athlete or a beginner on your fitness journey, this chapter will serve as a valuable resource, guiding you toward a healthier, more balanced lifestyle.

Chapter 01: Crossfit: High-Intensity Functional Training

Introduction to CrossFit

In this section, we delve into the dynamic world of CrossFit, a high-intensity functional training program that has redefined modern fitness. CrossFit combines high-intensity strength training, endurance exercises, and flexibility routines. Its essence lies in its focus on functional movements that mimic everyday activities, making it a practical approach for improving overall fitness and day-to-day physical performance.

CrossFit workouts, known as WODs (Workouts of the Day), are designed to be varied and challenging. They incorporate elements from weightlifting, gymnastics, and cardiovascular training. This diversity ensures that no two workouts are the same, keeping participants engaged and motivated. The core principle of CrossFit is to perform these functional movements at a high intensity, aiming to push individuals to their limits and promote continuous improvement.

Benefits of CrossFit

CrossFit offers many benefits, making it a highly appealing fitness program for individuals of all ages and fitness levels. Here are some of the primary advantages:

Increased Strength

One of the most significant benefits of CrossFit is the increase in muscular strength. The program's emphasis on weightlifting and resistance training helps build muscle mass and enhance overall strength. Exercises such as deadlifts, squats, and presses target major muscle groups, promoting balanced muscular development and functional strength.

Cardiovascular Fitness

CrossFit's high-intensity workouts provide an excellent cardiovascular workout. Combining aerobic exercises like running and rowing with strength training increases heart rate, improving cardiovascular health and endurance. Over time, regular participation in CrossFit can lead to better heart health and increased stamina.

Improved Body Composition

CrossFit is highly effective for those looking to improve their body composition. The intense, full-body workouts boost metabolic rate, leading to more significant calorie expenditure during and after exercise.

The boost in your metabolic rate increases fat loss and the development of lean muscle mass, contributing to a more toned and athletic physique.

Supportive Community Environment

A unique aspect of CrossFit is its strong sense of community. CrossFit gyms, or "boxes," foster a supportive and motivating environment where individuals encourage each other to reach their fitness goals. This camaraderie creates a positive and inclusive atmosphere, helping participants stay committed and enjoy their fitness journey.

Risks and Considerations

While CrossFit offers numerous benefits, it is essential to be aware of the potential risks and considerations associated with this high-intensity training program.

Risk of Overtraining

CrossFit's intense workouts can sometimes lead to overtraining if proper rest and recovery are not prioritized. Overtraining can result in fatigue, decreased performance, and an increased risk of injuries. To mitigate this risk, listening to your body, incorporating rest days, and ensuring adequate sleep and nutrition are crucial.

Injuries

CrossFit's high-intensity and complex movements can pose a risk of injuries, mainly if exercises are performed incorrectly or with excessive weight. Common injuries include strains, sprains, and joint issues. To minimize these risks, prioritize proper technique, gradually increase workout intensity, and seek guidance from certified CrossFit coaches who can provide individualized instruction and correction.

Importance of Proper Form and Progression

Proper form during CrossFit exercises is essential to prevent injuries and maximize effectiveness. Beginners should focus on mastering basic movements before progressing to more advanced techniques. CrossFit coaches play a vital role in ensuring participants use correct form and progress safely and appropriately, tailoring workouts to individual capabilities and goals.

Sample CrossFit Routines

To help you get started with CrossFit, here are some practical examples of CrossFit routines tailored to different fitness levels. These routines demonstrate the structure and variety typical of CrossFit workouts, showcasing how to design a well-rounded session.

Beginner Routine

1. **Warm-Up**: 5 minutes of light cardio (jump rope, jogging, etc.)
2. **Skill Practice**: 10 minutes of air squats and push-ups
3. **WOD**:
     - 10 minutes AMRAP (As Many Rounds As Possible)
          - 5 Push-Ups
          - 10 Air Squats
          - 15 Sit-Ups
4. **Cool Down**: 5 minutes of stretching and mobility exercises

This routine focuses on foundational movements, providing a solid introduction to CrossFit while building strength and endurance.

Intermediate Routine

1. **Warm-Up**: 5 minutes of dynamic stretching and mobility work
2. **Skill Practice**: 10 minutes practicing kettlebell swings and box jumps
3. **WOD**:
    - 15 minutes AMRAP
        - 10 Kettlebell Swings (35 lbs/16 kg)
        - 15 Box Jumps (20 inches)
        - 20 Wall Balls (14 lbs/6 kg)
4. **Cool Down**: 10 minutes of foam rolling and static stretching

This routine introduces more complex movements and a longer workout duration, challenging participants to improve their cardiovascular fitness and muscular endurance.

Advanced Routine

1. **Warm-Up**: 10 minutes of mixed cardio and mobility drills
2. **Skill Practice**: 15 minutes practicing clean and jerks
3. **WOD**:
    - 20 minutes EMOM (Every Minute On the Minute)
        - Minute 1: 15 Thrusters (95 lbs/43 kg)
        - Minute 2: 15 Pull-Ups
        - Minute 3: 15 Burpees
        - Repeat the cycle for 20 minutes
4. **Cool Down**: 10-15 minutes of yoga and deep stretching

This advanced routine incorporates high-intensity, full-body exercises that require strength, coordination, and endurance. The EMOM format ensures that participants maintain high effort throughout the workout.

These sample routines illustrate CrossFit's flexibility and scalability. It allows individuals to tailor their workouts to their fitness levels and goals. CrossFit is an engaging and effective way to improve overall fitness and well-being by incorporating various exercises and formats.

Chapter 02: Olympic Weightlifting: Strength and Precision

Understanding Olympic Weightlifting

Olympic weightlifting is a sport that epitomizes the fusion of strength, power, and technical precision. Unlike other forms of weightlifting, Olympic lifting focuses on two primary lifts: the snatch and the clean and jerk. These lifts require not only raw power but also an extraordinary level of coordination, balance, and flexibility.

The Snatch

The snatch is a lift where the athlete lifts the barbell from the ground to overhead in one fluid motion. It is a highly technical lift that demands speed, precision, and flexibility. The snatch is performed by grasping the barbell with a wide grip, pulling it from the floor, and explosively extending the hips and knees to propel the bar overhead. The lift is complete when the lifter catches the bar in a deep squat position and then stands up with the bar overhead.

The Clean and Jerk

The clean and jerk are two-part lifts. In the clean, the athlete pulls the barbell from the ground to the shoulders in one explosive movement, catching it in a squat position. In the jerk, the lifter then drives the barbell overhead by utilizing the legs and shoulders, splitting or pushing their feet apart to stabilize the weight overhead. This lift combines strength, power, and agility, making it a comprehensive test of the athlete's abilities.

Benefits of Olympic Weightlifting

Olympic weightlifting offers many benefits beyond the competitive arena, making it a valuable addition to any fitness regimen.

Increased Explosive Power

One of the primary benefits of Olympic weightlifting is the development of explosive power. The nature of the lifts requires rapid force production, which enhances the body's ability to generate power quickly. This attribute benefits weightlifting and various sports and physical activities requiring quick, powerful movements.

Full-Body Strength Development

Olympic weightlifting engages multiple muscle groups simultaneously, promoting comprehensive strength development. The snatch and clean & jerk work the legs, hips, back, shoulders, and arms, providing a full-body workout that builds functional strength. This holistic approach to strength training helps improve overall physical performance and resilience.

Improved Body Composition

Regular participation in Olympic weightlifting can lead to significant improvements in body composition. The high-intensity nature of the lifts increases metabolic rate, promoting fat loss while building lean muscle mass. This style of weightlifting results in a more toned and athletic physique, enhancing both aesthetics and physical capabilities.

Risks and Considerations

While Olympic weightlifting offers numerous benefits, it is essential to acknowledge and address the potential risks associated with the sport.

Injury Due to Improper Technique

The technical complexity of Olympic weightlifting means improper technique can lead to injuries. Common injuries include strains, sprains, and joint issues, particularly in the shoulders, knees, and lower back.

Proper form and technique, especially when lifting heavy weights, are prioritized to mitigate the risk of injury.

Importance of Proper Coaching

Proper coaching is vital in Olympic weightlifting. A knowledgeable coach can provide guidance on technique, help identify and correct errors, and design appropriate training programs. Coaching ensures that lifters progress safely and effectively, minimizing the risk of injury and maximizing performance gains.

Gradual Progression

Gradual progression is critical to success in Olympic weightlifting. Lifters should focus on mastering the technique before increasing their weight. This approach allows the body to adapt to the demands of the sport, reducing the likelihood of overuse injuries and ensuring steady, sustainable progress.

Sample Weightlifting Routines

To help you incorporate Olympic weightlifting into your training regimen, here are some practical routines designed to improve technique and build strength. These routines include a variety of exercises that target different aspects of the lifts, promoting well-rounded development.

Beginner Routine

1. **Warm-Up**: 10 minutes of dynamic stretching and mobility work
2. **Technique Practice**:
    - Snatch Pulls: 3 sets of 5 reps (light weight)
    - Clean Pulls: 3 sets of 5 reps (light weight)
3. **Strength Training**:
    - Front Squats: 3 sets of 5 reps
    - Overhead Press: 3 sets of 5 reps
4. **Accessory Work**:
    - Romanian Deadlifts: 3 sets of 8 reps
    - Plank Holds: 3 sets of 1-minute
5. **Cool Down**: 10 minutes of static stretching

This beginner routine focuses on developing the foundational strength and technique for safe and effective weightlifting.

Intermediate Routine

1. **Warm-Up**: 15 minutes of dynamic stretching and foam rolling
2. **Technique Practice**:
    - Hang Snatches: 4 sets of 3 reps
    - Power Cleans: 4 sets of 3 reps
3. **Strength Training**:
    - Back Squats: 4 sets of 5 reps
    - Push Press: 4 sets of 5 reps
4. **Accessory Work**:
    - Pull-Ups: 3 sets of 8 reps
    - Russian Twists: 3 sets of 20 reps
5. **Cool Down**: 10-15 minutes of yoga and mobility exercises

The intermediate routine builds on the foundational skills, incorporating more complex lifts and increasing the intensity of the workouts.

Advanced Routine

1. **Warm-Up**: 15-20 minutes of comprehensive mobility work and activation exercises
2. **Technique Practice**:
    - Full Snatches: 5 sets of 2 reps
    - Clean and Jerks: 5 sets of 2 reps
3. **Strength Training**:
    - Deadlifts: 4 sets of 5 reps
    - Bench Press: 4 sets of 5 reps
4. **Accessory Work**:
    - Bulgarian Split Squats: 3 sets of 8 reps per leg
    - Hanging Leg Raises: 3 sets of 15 reps

5. **Cool Down**: 15-20 minutes of deep stretching and foam rolling

The advanced routine outlined above is for experienced lifters. It focuses on refining techniques and maximizing strength gains through high-intensity, compound movements.

By incorporating these sample routines into your training, you can develop the strength, power, and technical precision required for Olympic weightlifting. Remember to prioritize proper form, seek guidance from a qualified coach, and progress gradually to ensure safe and practical training.

Chapter 03: Yoga: Mindful Movement and Flexibility

Introduction to Yoga

Yoga is a holistic practice integrating physical postures (asanas), breathing techniques (pranayama), and mindfulness to promote overall well-being. With historical roots tracing over 5,000 years to ancient India, yoga has evolved into various styles and forms, each offering unique benefits. This practice emphasizes the connection between the mind, body, and spirit, fostering balance and harmony.

Historical Roots

The origins of yoga are deeply embedded in ancient India's spiritual and philosophical traditions. The earliest references to yoga are found in the Rig Veda, an ancient collection of texts. Over time, yoga was refined and systematized by various sages and philosophers, most notably Patanjali, who compiled the Yoga Sutras around 400 CE. These texts provide a comprehensive guide to the theory and practice of yoga, outlining the Eight Limbs of Yoga, which encompass ethical guidelines, physical postures, breath control, sensory withdrawal, concentration, meditation, and spiritual enlightenment.

Various Styles of Yoga

Yoga has branched into numerous styles, each catering to different needs and preferences. This diversity allows individuals to find a practice that resonates with their goals and physical capabilities. We will explore some of the most popular styles in detail to help you choose the right one for your needs.

Benefits of Yoga

Yoga offers a wide array of benefits that extend beyond physical fitness. Here are some of the most notable advantages:

Increased Flexibility

One of the most immediate and apparent benefits of yoga is increased flexibility. Regular practice helps lengthen and stretch muscles, enhancing overall flexibility and range of motion, alleviating stiffness, and reducing the risk of injuries.

Improved Balance

Yoga postures often require balance and coordination, strengthening the stabilizer muscles and improving overall body balance. Overall, body balance is particularly beneficial for older adults, helping to prevent falls and maintain independence.

Stress Reduction

Yoga incorporates mindfulness and deep breathing techniques that activate the parasympathetic nervous system, promoting relaxation and reducing stress. Practices like restorative yoga and yoga nidra are particularly effective for calming the mind and relieving tension.

Enhanced Mind-Body Awareness

Yoga fosters a deep connection between the mind and body, encouraging practitioners to tune into their physical sensations, thoughts, and emotions. This heightened awareness can lead to better self-understanding and more mindful living.

Styles of Yoga

There are many styles of yoga, each with its unique approach and benefits. Here, we will explore some of the most popular styles to help you find the one that best suits your needs:

Hatha Yoga

Hatha yoga is a gentle and foundational style focusing on basic postures and breathing exercises. It is ideal for beginners as it provides a solid introduction to yoga, emphasizing alignment and mindful movement.

Vinyasa Yoga

Vinyasa yoga, also known as flow yoga, involves a dynamic sequence of poses synchronized with the breath. This style is more physically demanding than Hatha yoga and is suitable for a more vigorous workout that improves strength and cardiovascular health.

Bikram Yoga

Bikram yoga, also known as hot yoga, consists of a specific sequence of 26 postures and two breathing exercises performed in a heated room. The heat enhances flexibility and detoxification through sweating, making it a challenging but rewarding practice.

Yin Yoga

Yin yoga is a slow-paced style that involves holding passive poses for extended periods, typically 3-5 minutes. This practice targets the deep connective tissues, promoting flexibility and joint mobility. It is especially beneficial for stress relief and mindfulness.

Sample Yoga Routines

To help you incorporate yoga into your daily routine, here are some practical yoga routines designed to achieve various goals:

Enhancing Flexibility

1. **Warm-Up**: 5 minutes of gentle stretches (e.g., neck rolls, shoulder shrugs)
2. **Main Sequence**:
   - Cat-Cow Pose: 5 breaths
   - Downward-Facing Dog: 5 breaths
   - Standing Forward Bend: 5 breaths
   - Low Lunge: 5 breaths on each side
   - Seated Forward Bend: 5 breaths
   - Butterfly Pose: 5 breaths
   - Reclining Pigeon Pose: 5 breaths on each side

3. **Cool Down**: 5 minutes of deep breathing in Savasana (Corpse Pose)

Reducing Stress

1. **Warm-Up**: 5 minutes of deep breathing (e.g., Ujjayi breath)
2. **Main Sequence**:
    - Child's Pose: 5 minutes
    - Supported Bridge Pose: 5 minutes
    - Legs-Up-The-Wall Pose: 5 minutes
    - Supine Twist: 5 breaths on each side
    - Restorative Forward Bend: 5 minutes
3. **Cool Down**: 10 minutes of guided meditation or yoga nidra

Building Strength

1. **Warm-Up**: 5 minutes of sun salutations
2. **Main Sequence**:
    - Plank Pose: 1 minute
    - Four-Limbed Staff Pose (Chaturanga): 5 reps
    - Warrior I: 5 breaths on each side
    - Warrior II: 5 breaths on each side
    - Boat Pose: 5 breaths
    - Crow Pose: 5 breaths
    - Side Plank: 5 breaths on each side
3. **Cool Down**: 5 minutes of stretching (e.g., seated forward bend, happy baby pose)

These sample routines cater to different goals and experience levels, providing a structured approach to incorporating yoga into your life. Whether you seek to enhance flexibility, reduce stress, or build strength, yoga offers a versatile and holistic practice supporting physical and mental well-being.

Chapter 04: Energize Every Fiber Stretch Sample

Energize Every Fiber (Ebook Sample)

Purchase Full Ebook at FuelMinds.Academy

* * *

Core and Back Flexibility Street

Core and back flexibility are crucial for overall body function and injury prevention. This chapter provides detailed instructions on specific stretches that target these areas, improving flexibility, reducing tension, and enhancing spinal alignment. These exercises include the Standing Side Stretch, Cat-Cow Pose, and Child's Pose, each tailored to maximize the benefits for the core and back.

Standing Side Stretch: Execution and Key Points for Stretching Side Muscles

Technique:

1. Stand with your feet shoulder-width apart and arms at your sides.

2. Raise your right arm overhead, reaching towards the ceiling.

3. Gently lean to the left, pushing your right hip out to the side to deepen the stretch along your right side.

4.Hold the stretch for 20-30 seconds, feeling a continuous stretch line from your right ankle to your fingertips.

5.Return to the upright position and repeat on the opposite side with your left arm raised and leaning to the right.

Key Points:

1. Ensure your hips remain aligned and facing forward; avoid twisting your torso.

2. Keep your raised arm close to your ear to maximize the stretch down your side.

3. Breathe deeply, using your breath to expand the ribs and enhance the stretch.

Cat-Cow Pose: Flow Sequence for Spinal Health

Technique:

1. Begin on your hands and knees, with your wrists aligned under your shoulders and your knees under your hips.

2. Inhale as you arch your back downwards, lifting your head and tailbone towards the ceiling (Cow Pose).

3. Exhale as you round your back upwards, tucking your chin to your chest and curling your tailbone under (Cat Pose).

4. Continue flowing between these two positions for 1-2 minutes, synchronizing your movement with your breath.

Benefits: This flow sequence promotes spinal flexibility and relieves neck, shoulders, and lower back tension. Regular practice can also help improve posture and balance by strengthening the abdominal and back muscles.

Child's Pose: Proper Form and Its Soothing Effects on the Back and Mind

Technique:

1. Start on your knees with your big toes touching and knees hip-width apart.

2. Sit back on your heels and fold forward, extending your arms in front of you on the floor.

3. Lower your forehead to the ground, letting your entire body relax.

4. Hold this position for 30 seconds to a few minutes, focusing on deep, slow breaths.

Proper Form:

1. Ensure your hips remain over your heels as you stretch forward.

2. Spread your knees wider for a deeper hip stretch or keep them closer for more support.

3. Extend your arms forward to lengthen the spine or place them alongside your body for a more restful pose.

Soothing Effects:

Child's Pose is a restorative stretch that helps release back, shoulders, and neck tension while calming the mind. It's often used as a pose of rest between more challenging poses during yoga practice. The pose's forward folded and grounding nature also helps alleviate stress and anxiety, making it beneficial for mental well-being.

These stretches are designed to improve physical flexibility and enhance mental relaxation and stress relief. Integrating these exercises into your routine allows you to achieve greater mobility in the core and back, which is crucial for a healthy posture and efficient movement.

Chapter 05: Meditation and Breathing Exercises in Daily Fitness

Integrating Meditation and Mindfulness

Incorporating meditation and mindfulness into your daily fitness routine can enhance overall well-being. These practices involve focusing your attention and eliminating the stream of jumbled thoughts that may crowd your mind, promoting a state of tranquility and clarity. Integrating meditation and mindfulness with physical exercise can cultivate a deeper connection between your mind and body, improve your mental health, and optimize your physical performance.

The Significance of Meditation and Mindfulness

Meditation and mindfulness are not merely passive activities but active practices. Meditation involves focusing inwardly, often through guided sessions, mantras, or breathing exercises. On the other hand, mindfulness is the practice of being fully present and engaged in the current moment. These practices help reduce stress, enhance concentration, and foster greater well-being.

Benefits of Meditation and Breathing Exercises

Meditation and breathing exercises offer many mental and physical benefits that significantly enhance your fitness journey.

Reduced Stress

One of the most well-known benefits of meditation is its ability to reduce stress. By engaging in regular meditation, you activate the body's relaxation response, which lowers cortisol levels and alleviates stress. Reduced stress levels lead to improved mental clarity, better sleep, and a more positive outlook.

Improved Focus

Meditation enhances your ability to concentrate by training your mind to stay present. This improved focus can translate to better workout performance, allowing you to execute exercises more precisely and effectively. Additionally, enhanced focus can improve productivity and cognitive function in other areas of your life.

Emotional Regulation

Regular meditation helps regulate emotions by promoting a greater awareness of thoughts and feelings. This heightened awareness allows you to respond to emotions more effectively than impulsively. Emotional regulation is crucial for maintaining motivation and consistency in your fitness routine and overall mental health.

Incorporating Mindfulness into Workouts

The quality and enjoyment of your workouts are only enhanced when you seamlessly integrate mindfulness into your fitness routine. Here are some practical ways to incorporate mindfulness techniques into your exercise regimen.

Breath Awareness

Focusing on your breath is a simple yet powerful mindfulness technique. By paying attention to your breathing, you can stay present and connected to your body, improving your exercise form and reducing the risk of injury.

Step-by-Step Guide for Breath Awareness

1. **Begin with a Centering Breath**: Take a few moments to center yourself before starting your workout. Sit or stand comfortably, close your eyes, and take a deep breath through your nose, allowing your abdomen to expand. Exhale slowly through your mouth, releasing any tension.
2. **Focus on Your Breath During Exercise**: Throughout your workout, maintain an awareness of your breathing. Notice the rhythm of your breath and how it changes with different exercises. For example, focus on taking deep, steady breaths during cardio exercises to sustain energy levels.
3. **Use Breath to Enhance Movement**: Coordinate your breath with your movements. Inhale during the preparatory phase of an exercise and exhale during the exertion phase. For instance, inhale as you lower into a squat and exhale as you rise. This technique helps you stay present and perform exercises more efficiently.

Mindful Movement

Mindful movement involves paying close attention to the sensations in your body as you exercise. This practice encourages you to move with intention and awareness, improving your connection to your body and enhancing your overall workout experience.

Step-by-Step Guide for Mindful Movement

1. **Set an Intention**: At the beginning of your workout, set an intention for your practice. Focus on form, breathe, or enjoy the movement. Setting an intention helps direct your attention and keeps you engaged.
2. **Tune Into Your Body**: Regularly check in with your body as you work out. Notice how your muscles feel, the alignment of your joints, and any areas of tension or discomfort. Adjust your movements as needed to maintain proper form and prevent injury.
3. **Stay Present**: Keep your mind focused on the present moment. If you notice your thoughts wandering, gently bring your attention back to your breath or the sensations in your body. Returning to the present moment strengthens your mindfulness skills over time.

Guided Meditation Post-Workout

A short guided meditation session after your workout can enhance recovery and promote relaxation. This practice helps calm the mind, reduce muscle tension, and improve overall recovery.

Step-by-Step Guide for Post-Workout Meditation

1. **Find a Comfortable Position**: After completing your workout, find a comfortable seated or lying position. Close your eyes and take a few deep breaths to settle your mind and body.

2. **Focus on Your Breath**: Bring your attention to your breath, inhaling deeply through your nose and exhaling slowly through your mouth. Allow your breath to become natural and effortless.

3. **Guided Visualization**: A guided meditation app or recording will lead you through a short visualization. Imagine a peaceful place, such as a beach or forest, and visualize yourself there, experiencing a sense of calm and relaxation.

4. **Body Scan**: Perform a body scan by focusing on different body parts, starting from your toes and moving up to your head. Notice any areas of tension and consciously relax those muscles.

5. **Closing**: Finish your meditation by taking a few deep breaths and gently opening your eyes. Take a moment to notice how you feel before moving on with your day.

Integrating meditation and mindfulness into your fitness routine can enhance your physical and mental well-being. These practices promote a deeper connection to your body, reduce stress, and improve overall performance, making them valuable components of a holistic fitness regimen.

6 |

Conclusion

Holistic Wellness Through Movement and Mindfulness

In this phase, we have explored various fitness and wellness practices, each offering unique benefits that contribute to a holistic approach to well-being. By embracing high-intensity training, weightlifting, yoga, and mindfulness, individuals can cultivate a balanced and integrated fitness regimen that promotes physical strength, mental clarity, and emotional balance.

Embracing High-Intensity Training

High-intensity training, exemplified by CrossFit, offers a powerful way to enhance cardiovascular health, build muscular strength, and improve overall fitness. These dynamic and varied workouts keep the body and mind engaged, preventing monotony and promoting continuous improvement. Through high-intensity functional training, individuals can push their limits, achieve new personal bests, and experience the thrill of physical challenge and accomplishment.

The Power of Weightlifting

Olympic weightlifting brings a unique dimension to fitness with its emphasis on strength, power, and precision. The technical nature of the snatch and clean & jerk fosters discipline and focus, while the full-body engagement builds robust muscular development and functional strength. Weightlifting transforms the body and enhances mental resilience as lifters learn to overcome challenges and set incremental goals. By incorporating weightlifting into their fitness routines, individuals can achieve a harmonious balance of strength, power, and technique.

The Harmony of Yoga

Yoga offers a counterbalance to the intensity of weightlifting and high-intensity training, focusing on flexibility, balance, and mindfulness. Yoga fosters a deep connection between the mind and body, promoting relaxation and stress relief. Through various styles, such as Hatha, Vinyasa, Bikram, and Yin, yoga caters to diverse needs and preferences, providing a path to enhanced physical and mental well-being. Regular yoga practice cultivates flexibility, improves balance, and nurtures a sense of inner peace and calm.

Integrating Mindfulness and Meditation

Mindfulness and meditation are essential components of a holistic fitness regimen. These practices enhance mental clarity, reduce stress, and improve emotional regulation. By integrating mindfulness techniques into workouts and dedicating time to meditation, individuals can connect more with their bodies and minds. Breath awareness, mindful movement, and post-workout meditation create a well-rounded approach to fitness that supports overall health and well-being.

Cultivating Holistic Well-Being

By weaving together these diverse fitness and wellness practices, individuals can cultivate a holistic approach to well-being. High-intensity training, weightlifting, yoga, and mindfulness each contribute unique benefits, creating a comprehensive fitness regimen that addresses all aspects of health. This integrated approach promotes physical strength, mental clarity, and emotional balance, enabling individuals to thrive in all areas of life.

Embracing a holistic fitness routine requires commitment, self-awareness, and a willingness to explore different practices. It is essential to listen to your body, set realistic goals, and seek guidance from qualified coaches and instructors. Doing so can create a personalized fitness journey that evolves with your needs and objectives, fostering long-term health and happiness.

Final Thoughts

In conclusion, the path to holistic wellness paves the way for diverse and enriching practices that nurture the body, mind, and spirit. High-intensity training challenges the body, weightlifting builds strength and power, yoga fosters flexibility and mindfulness, and meditation cultivates mental clarity and emotional balance. By embracing these practices, you can achieve a state of holistic well-being that empowers you to live a vibrant, healthy, and fulfilling life.

Remember, the journey to holistic wellness is a lifelong endeavor. Stay curious and committed, and enjoy discovering what makes you feel strong, balanced, and whole. Your dedication to movement and mindfulness will yield profound benefits, enhancing every aspect of your life and helping you become the best version of yourself.